THE WORLD'S CITIES

LONDON

CREDITS

Series Editor: Nicolas Wright
Series Designer: Kris Flynn
Picture Researcher: Kathy Brandt

Text by Tony Aldous

Commissioned Photographs by
Robin Bath

Published by Chartwell Books Inc., A
Division of Book Sales Inc., 110 Enterprise
Avenue, Secaucus, New Jersey 07094

Produced by Theorem Publishing Limited,
71/73 Great Portland Street, London W1N 5DH
for Marshall Cavendish Books Limited

Printed in Great Britain

First printing 1978

ISBN 0 89009 159 5

THE WORLD'S CITIES

LONDON

CHARTWELL
BOOKS INC.

CONTENTS

Introduction to London

Thirty years ago the school textbooks used by London children boasted that their blitzed and blackened city was 'the greatest' in the world. Greatest meant biggest in population; it meant biggest in area; and it implied also that London was still then the heart of a great and glorious empire.

Today London is no longer 'greatest' in any of these senses. The British have given away most of their empire; London's population, partly as a result of deliberate policies, has fallen from its 1950s peak of nearly eight and a half million to fewer than seven million; and half a dozen cities in Asia and the Third World have far outstripped it in numbers and area.

Yet London remains in many ways the outstanding 'world city'. It may no longer rule an empire, but it remains a formidable commercial force. The expertise of its commodity markets and its international insurance and banking organisations give its historic commercial centre, 'The City', a rare status.

Another way in which three decades have transformed London is in mood. It is altogether livelier and more attractive. People visit it not, as in its imperial heyday, because they felt compelled to, they come because they like the place.

And this stems only partly from the informality and innovation that won 1960s London its 'swinging' reputation. There is much more to it than that. Many American visitors say they find London the most 'livable' of the world's big cities. You can still walk about the streets comfortably and securely. It has its share of new tower blocks, new highways and restless, fast moving traffic. But they have not destroyed its unique character and atmosphere.

It is still possible to wander in spacious parkland so lush that traffic noise is a forgotten, distant rumble; to stroll through elegant 18th and 19th-century streets where rectilinear steel, plate-glass and concrete seem not to exist. A block away, round a couple of corners, they reappear in a comfortable, convenient tourist hotel — but for the most part not too obtrusively.

Perhaps this is the key to London's popularity. It retains great diversity. It is cosmopolitan, so that the visitor does not feel isolated. It is on the whole friendly — Londoners will generally take time and trouble to help a stranger. And when it comes to things to do, the richness of what it has to offer in fields like theatre, music, museums, art galleries, and sport, withstand challenge from any other city anywhere in the world.

Despite the bulldozer, despite too many motorcars, despite the stops and goes of an erratic economy, London has flourished and blossomed with an amazing richness. It was a Scotsman, William Dunbar, who wrote nearly 500 years ago, 'London, thou art the flower of cities all!'. Its 1970s bloom is richer than ever.

REGENTS PARK

EUSTON RD.

TOTTENHAM COURT RD.

BAKER ST.

OXFORD ST.

1

3

HAYMARKET

BAYSWATER RD.

HYDE PARK

PARK LANE

THE SERPENTINE

PICCADILLY

ROTTEN ROW

GREEN PARK

THE MALL

ST. JAMES'S
PARK

KNIGHTSBRIDGE

BUCKINGHAM
PALACE
GARDENS

BIRDCAGE WALK

SLOANE ST.

2

4

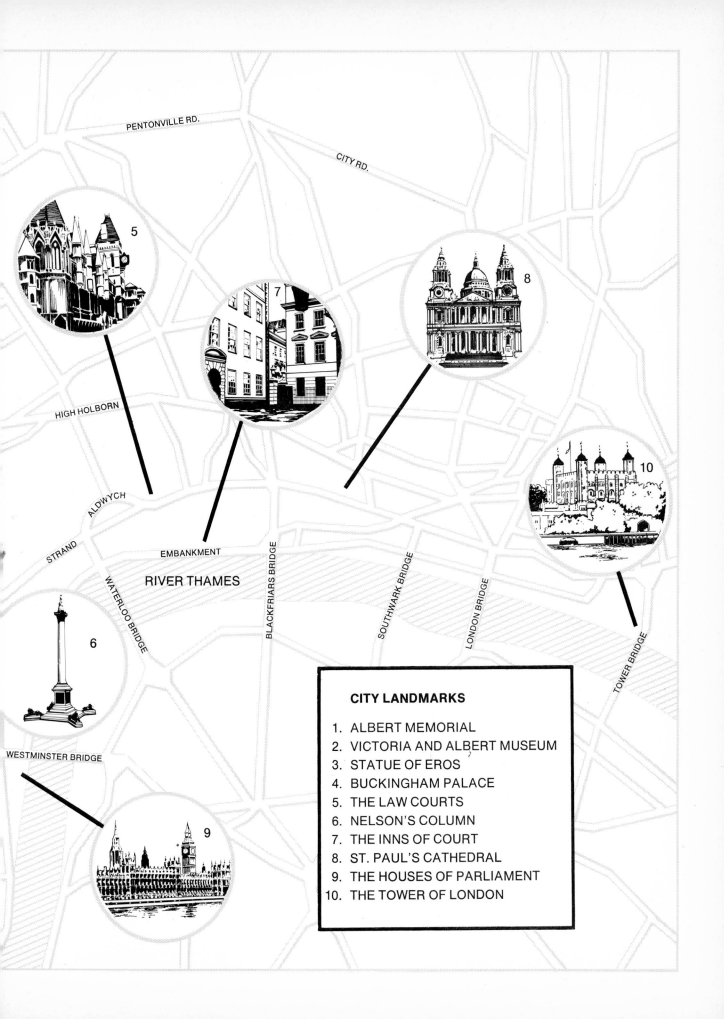

PENTONVILLE RD.

CITY RD.

HIGH HOLBORN

ALDWYCH

STRAND

EMBANKMENT

RIVER THAMES

WATERLOO BRIDGE

BLACKFRIARS BRIDGE

SOUTHWARK BRIDGE

LONDON BRIDGE

TOWER BRIDGE

WESTMINSTER BRIDGE

CITY LANDMARKS

1. ALBERT MEMORIAL
2. VICTORIA AND ALBERT MUSEUM
3. STATUE OF EROS
4. BUCKINGHAM PALACE
5. THE LAW COURTS
6. NELSON'S COLUMN
7. THE INNS OF COURT
8. ST. PAUL'S CATHEDRAL
9. THE HOUSES OF PARLIAMENT
10. THE TOWER OF LONDON

London As It Was

London first became a city under the Romans, following a successful invasion of southern Britain by the Emperor Claudius in AD 50. A kind of settlement had already grown up there because this was the lowest point at which the Thames could be easily forded.

The Romans were quick to realize the site's potential and built the first London Bridge. From this early wooden structure radiated their roads: Watling Street south-eastwards to the Channel ports and north-west towards Chester; Ermine Street north towards York and south to Chichester; Ealde Street eastwards to Colchester, then a much more important town than London.

The original Roman town, Londinium, was also wooden until, in AD 60 Boadicea, Queen of the Iceni, rebelled against Roman rule. She burnt and pillaged both Colchester and London before the legions could be recalled from the north to suppress the revolt. After that the Romans rebuilt Londinium in stone.

Because of its position as crossroads and crossing place as well as a port, Londinium became the largest city in the western part of the Roman Empire. But after the Romans left in AD 410, the city entered the Dark Ages: its grand buildings fell into disrepair and the settlement that remained suffered sacking and burning at the hands of successive waves of invaders from continental Europe. Yet, if Greater London, the present city of almost seven million people, is essentially a city of villages, then most of those villages owe their origin to bands of marauding Saxons who decided to settle down.

London, from the fifth to the 11th centuries, was not England's capital city. Indeed there was no England until a Saxon King, Alfred the Great of Wessex, united the Saxons and pushed the Danes back in AD 877 into the northern and eastern parts of the country. His capital was Winchester. The city of London and most of its surroundings were strongly Saxon; but the eastern parts of what is now Greater London, north of the Thames, lay inside the Danelaw, on Danish territory.

Under Alfred, London rebuilt its walls, formed a militia, and began to establish the makings of civic independence. The later Saxon kings were mostly crowned at Kingston (the King's town), 12 miles south-west from London Bridge but today also in Greater London. The city within its walls, however, grew more and more prosperous and powerful. By 1042 when Canute died and the Witan (or council of wise men) met to decide on a successor, representatives of the City of London had a dominant voice in the proceedings that restored the Saxon line, with Edward the Confessor as king.

Edward's reign saw the rebuilding of an abbey one-and-a-quarter miles west of the walled city. Alongside this abbey, the West Minster, he built a royal palace. Thus began the twin centres of modern London: the City, the business capital; Westminster, the royal and administrative capital. Indeed for another six centuries the two

Tower Bridge, despite its gothic appearance, is a 19th-century steel-framed structure. It still opens to let large ships go up river.

remained physically separate, with only a sprinkling of palaces and grand houses overlooking the strand in between. And, although London is today for strategic purposes administered by the Greater London Council, the traditional duality of its centre is still reflected in the names of two of its local authorities: the City of London and the City of Westminster.

In 1066 England was successfully invaded for the last time by a foreign army: the Normans under their duke, William. He defeated Harold, whose succession he disputed, at Hastings on the south-east coast and marched to London. If he expected the citizens to fling open the gates in joy, he was mistaken; and walled London beyond the Thames was sufficiently formidable a fortress for him to turn away at Southwark and cross the Thames higher up.

By the time he came back that Christmas on the eve of his coronation, their attitude had changed. Norman rule was now an indisputable fact; perhaps there had been some parleying? The city proclaimed him king, and in return for their support and loyalty, its inhabitants received all the civic privileges and more that they had enjoyed in good King Edward's day.

But William the Conqueror was also William the prudent! He set about building a stone castle adjoining and looking over the city's eastern wall. It stands today. Known as the White Tower, it forms the central keep of that impressive, noble, three-ring concentric fortress, the Tower of London.

Throughout most of the medieval period, London was twice as populous as any other English city and many times richer. While feudal power held sway in most of England, London's Lord Mayor and aldermen administered their own courts and maintained a formidable armed force in the city's trained militia. During the 12th-century civil war between King Stephen and his rival for the crown, Matilda, that queen gave the Constable of the Tower rule over the city. He found he could not enforce it, was soon Stephen's prisoner and had to cede the Tower in ransom. Stephen promptly restored all the city's rights.

In the 12th century when Richard I was crusading in the Holy Land, his regent, who had made the Tower his headquarters, provoked the citizens to revolt in favour of Prince John, the king's brother. John led the city militia to the Tower, besieged the regent and forced him to surrender the fortress. However, in 1215, when John had become king, he found the city's boot was on the other foot. The Mayor and merchants of London joined the barons in extorting from him that

historic guarantee of rights and privileges, *Magna Carta*. One factor that persuaded the king was the likelihood that, if he did not agree, the citizenry would once again seize the Tower.

Increasingly, too, London's wealth told. Its merchants, no doubt, were only common men, who must bow, doff caps and show all respect to the landed nobility, but unlike landed magnates, they disposed of substantial liquid assets—not great estates—but gold and silver. So if the king lacked cash to pay an army or build a palace, he looked to London; London, respectfully but firmly, insisted on its price, often in new commercial privileges. In consequence, it grew steadily richer and more powerful.

By Shakespeare's day in the 16th century the city had spread westwards well beyond its walls; so had the authority of the Lord Mayor and aldermen. At Temple Bar a barrier set up across Fleet Street marked the limit of their jurisdiction. A later arch, designed by Sir Christopher Wren and dating from 1672, was moved to ease traffic congestion in the 1870s. It stands, now much decayed, at Theobalds Park, north-east of London. However, because it symbolizes constitutional freedom and the rule of law in both England and America, moves are afoot to restore and reinstate it in the City of London, perhaps on a site near St Paul's Cathedral. When the Queen visits the City, she still halts at its boundary with Westminster, where Temple Bar stood. The Lord Mayor proffers her the City's ceremonial sword which she accepts but hands back into his safekeeping— symbolizing the City's ancient independence under the Crown.

Left: The Houses of Parliament from the Thames. The big tower is the Victoria Tower; the clock tower is popularly known as 'Big Ben' after its bell.
Top: A Yeoman of the Guard, popularly known as a Beefeater, one of the guardians of the Tower of London, in his 16th century uniform.
Right: Temple Bar, which used to mark the entrance from Westminster into the historic City of London.

Left: London Bridge as it was in the 15th and 16th centuries. Until the 18th century this was London's only bridge across the Thames.
Below: The Ivory House, St Katharine's Dock. As larger vessels and automation have moved the Port down river, London has looked for new uses for its old docks. St Katharine's now serves as a yacht marina. This former ivory warehouse houses luxury apartments, shops, restaurants, and a yacht club.

London, in Shakespeare's time, had also spread to Southwark on the south bank. In 1550 its jurisdiction was extended to most of this area. London's purchase of lands from the church did not, however, include two areas known as the Liberties of Clink and Paris Garden. That is why many pleasure gardens, places of entertainment and, above all, theatres flourished there, outside the grasp of the City Corporation.

The bridge itself, many times destroyed and rebuilt since the Romans' original wooden structure, was by this time the 13th-century London Bridge of Peter de Colechurch—a stone construction of 20 gothic arches, almost 600 feet long and more than 20 feet wide. It had a double drawbridge, raised to let ships sail up river and keep intruders out of the city. On it, and cantilevered outwards, Londoners had built their houses of three, four and more storeys. Skewered on spikes at its Southwark end, the heads of traitors and criminals stood as a warning to the populace to be loyal and law-abiding.

Two later London bridges have followed: Rennie's graceful five-arch affair of 1831, whose stone façades at least now adorn a bridge at Lake Havasu City, Arizona; and the present, efficient but uninspiring structure opened in 1973.

Seventeenth-century London, though it had spread beyond the walls, was packed tight. The wealthier citizens might take to living in country villages like Kensington, coming in by carriage or on horseback. The poor, lacking any public transport, or the time or money to indulge in it had it existed, lived crammed together within or close under the walls. The importance then of living near your business is well demonstrated by the legal profession. Its private walled city, the Temple, stood on the eastern edge of the City of London, close both to trade and to the Court, Parliament and royal courts at Westminster. By the end of Queen Elizabeth's reign in 1603, 300000 people lived within or close to the Square Mile of the walled city. Sixty years later, when Samuel Pepys was writing his diary, the population and overcrowding had grown immeasurably, and were a contributing cause of the Great Plague of 1665. So too had congestion grown. Today's Londoners may complain of the occasional traffic jam in the Strand; they experience nothing like the total standstills which encouraged Pepys to take to the river as the fastest way of commuting between Westminster and the City.

By Pepys's time London had ceased for practical purposes to be a walled city. In the Civil War which culminated in Parliament's victory over Charles I, and ultimately the king's trial and execution, the Lord Mayor and aldermen had significantly ordered construction of a ring of defensive earthworks to protect both the City *and Westminster*.

The Great Plague of London and the Great Fire which followed it in 1666 demonstrated that bursting medieval London could no longer safely support all the activity crammed into it. Overcrowded wooden houses harboured the rats that carried the plague-spreading fleas. The plague virtually stopped the city's heart and by September 1665 the weekly death toll had reached 7000.

Fortunately the colder winter weather all but ended the plague and commercial life returned to normal — for a while! The next autumn those same wooden houses—crowded together in narrow lanes and alleys, their overhanging upper storeys often almost touching—caught a spark from a baker's oven in Pudding Lane, near London Bridge. The wind fanned the flames; citizens struggled to save their own possessions rather than quell the fire; and by the time the king's brother, the Duke of York, intervened by blowing up houses to make a fire break, four-fifths of London within the walls had perished.

The tragedy of the fire seemed to offer an opportunity to rebuild a spacious new City of London. Plans were not lacking. In reality, however, 17th-century London and England possessed neither the money nor the legal and administrative machinery to rebuild London in a new mould—least of all in the midst of an expensive war with the Dutch. The best it could do was rebuild on the old street lines, but in brick or stone rather than wood, with taller houses only on the wider streets and some street widening.

The great architect, Sir Christopher Wren, contributed to the rebuilding with a new St Paul's Cathedral and 49 city churches, most of which still survive today, though in some cases tucked away behind large new office blocks.

Seventeenth-century London also saw other significant changes. Thanks to a far-sighted citizen and engineer, Sir Hugh Myddelton, it

Below: Boadicia, Queen of the Iceni, rose against her Roman oppressors in AD 60 and captured and destroyed London. Her statue stands on the Victoria Embankment near Westminster Bridge.
Below right: Piccadilly Circus with traffic swirling round the statue of *Eros.*

gained, in the 38-mile-long New River, an aqueduct able to provide plentiful supplies of pure water in place of increasingly polluted Thames and well water.

The appearance of London was also changing. Inigo Jones's Whitehall Banqueting House and his Queen's House at Greenwich had given Londoners their first bemused taste of classical architecture instead of gothic. Now Wren and his contemporaries modified but reinforced the new fashion. For almost the next two centuries London's architecture—whether described as Jacobean, Queen Anne, Georgian or Victorian, and though usually a decade or two in advance of the rest of Britain—remained basically classical in style.

London continued to grow. The 17th century had seen planned development on the estates of the Earls and Dukes of Bedford at Covent Garden (originally the garden of a convent), the Earls of Southampton (Bloomsbury) and in the St James, Piccadilly and Soho areas. In the 18th century came the 'West End' — the planned and spacious Georgian grid development of Mayfair and Marylebone, culminating in the Regency period of the early 19th century with John Nash's grand design for a triumphal route via Regent Street and Portland Place, cutting through London to the landscaped green spaces and splendid stucco terraces of Regent's Park. Queen Anne's Gate, one of the prettiest and most complete 18th century streets in London, dates in part from 1704.

This century also did its best to improve the capital's road system. Westminster Bridge (1750) provided a second river crossing; Blackfriars (1769) and Battersea (1771) soon followed. The 'New Road' — along the line of what we now call City, Pentonville, Euston and Marylebone Roads—provided the city with its first major bypass and facilitated the rapid extension of the West End.

This was the London that prompted Dr Samuel Johnson (whose house you can still visit in Gough Square, just north of Fleet Street) to remark, 'When a man is tired of London, he is tired of life; for there is in London all that life can afford'.

And so there was for the rich, or even the tolerably well off. For the poor — ill-housed, ill-fed, constrained to exist in the ill-favoured areas where they could scratch, beg or steal a living — there was no escape until the railways came. For in the 19th century it was a transport revolution that produced the most dramatic changes of all in London's history. From the 1840s onwards the railways as well as horse omnibuses and later electric trams gave first the lower middle classes and then the working man, too, the chance to live in decent surroundings, with trees and gardens, rather than in overcrowded and improvized tenements.

The march of bricks and mortar went now at a phenomenal pace. In 1801 the population of London stood at about 800000; by 1851 it was more than two million; by 1901, four and a half million. By that time the fast-spreading underground railway system further encouraged commuting and in the 1920s and 1930s electrified suburban railways and surface extensions of the underground actually preceded and made possible the outward suburban sprawl. It had eaten up most of the historic county of Middlesex before any government cried halt. In 1931 the area we now call Greater London sheltered eight million people — more than one-sixth of the total United Kingdom population.

By this time London — commercial and political heart of a great empire — had developed a local government system to suit its size. First, in 1855, Parliament created the Metropolitan Board of Works to look after the needs of London outside the narrow boundaries of the historic city; then, in 1888, it set up the London County Council, covering some 74000 acres including the City. At the end of the century it added 28 metropolitan boroughs responsible, alongside the City Corporation, for more local matters.

The story of London in the 20th century has been of a pond with ever widening ripples. First London swallowed country villages like Islington; developers turned them into more or less favoured residential areas; their inhabitants then moved onward and outward, as better transport enabled then to commute further in pursuit of the receding countryside. Districts like Islington, Hackney and Camberwell lost favour and declined. Their grander houses were sub-divided; industry moved in. Congestion again threatened to choke the centre.

But already in the 1930s the London County Council had been buying agricultural land for a 'Green Belt' to halt the spread of the built-up areas. After the Second World War these policies were given legal effect as part of Britain's new planning system. But at the same time governments recognised that London was now too fat to be healthy. For the 30 years following the war they prescribed for the capital a deliberate 'slimming' regime. A ring of new towns beyond the Green Belt were built, to tempt industry and its workers to leave the capital, moulded on the example set by Ebenezer Howard's Welwyn

Left: The hotel front of St Pancras Station, high-watermark of 19th-century gothic architecture. An historic building protected by law, the station still functions as a main line terminus.

Above: How London's rapid 18th and 19th-century expansion appeared to one contemporary observer: 'The March of Bricks and Mortar' by George Cruishank.

Garden City of the 1920s. Londoners were entitled to the English
dream of an individual house with its own garden, said the planners.

The policy worked, partly because of the sticks and carrots of
government policy; partly because Londoners and London employers
were deciding to move out anyway to pleasanter and more profitable
pastures. In the last 20 years Greater London's population has fallen
from a peak of eight million to less than seven million. Partly because
of this, the city is a pleasanter place in which to live. Other factors that
make today's London more attractive to residents and visitors alike are
the cumulative effects of the 1956 Clean Air Act and other anti-
pollution measures; the cleaning up of the once badly polluted River
Thames, so that some 60 varieties of fish now live comfortably in its
waters; two new underground lines — The Victoria Line (completed
1971) and the Fleet Line (first section opened 1977); and a
computerised traffic control system which will eventually control
traffic lights at more than 1000 road junctions.

London's planners believed 15 years ago they could improve the
city's environment by bold and drastic change: ambitious new
highways cutting through the city; new flats in high white towers in
place of the Victorian brick terraces; people moved whether they liked
it or not from their familiar if substandard habitats to what the experts
thought best for them.

Right: The new Port of London is concentrated down-river, on wider, deeper reaches of the Thames, and uses modern cargo handling facilities like these at Tilbury.

That philosopy is now dead. London has neither the money nor the wish for large-scale drastic change. Conservation and gradual, cautious renewal are the watchwords. People's tastes have changed: affluent professional families have found that 19th-century inner suburbs like Islington offer roomy houses, attractive environments and short journeys to work and entertainment. Parts of the inner city are blooming.

But only parts. Departing industry has left uncomfortable gaps. The Port of London has, quite predictably but rather suddenly, moved down river to deeper, wider reaches of the Thames which can accommodate the new large bulk carrier ships. Much industry, often with the encouragement of government grants and inducements, has gone to other parts of the country where workers were more plentiful and communications less congested.

As a result, London and central government have once again changed their tune. They are now promoting the development of the inner city, and especially the 5000 acres of redundant dockland east of the City of London. One industry has, however, been booming: tourism. The capital now welcomes more than eight and a half million overseas visitors a year. Most of them arrive by air, either at Heathrow on the western edge of Greater London now linked by an underground extension with a train every four minutes, or to Gatwick in the south (already on a fast railway line) or to smaller airports at Luton, Stansted and Southend.

The main London airport, Heathrow, lies some 15 miles west of central London, to which it is joined by a spur from the main M4 London-South Wales Motorway. Heathrow was first developed as a civil airport in 1946, to replace the pre-war Croydon Aerodrome in south London whose runways were too short for modern aircraft. In the three decades since its foundation, Heathrow has never ceased growing, with some part or other of its huge area always the scene of building operations. Its central area, reached from the motorway by twin tunnels, now boasts three terminal buildings; a separate cargo terminal on the airport's southern edge connects to the centre by a second tunnel; while a third tunnel brings in an extension of the Piccadilly Line underground train to the newly completed Heathrow Central station. In peak summer periods the airport handles almost 1000 aircraft movements a day, with a plane landing or taking off every 1–2 minutes. Some 23 million passengers use Heathrow each year — the lion's share of the 32 million who pass through all five airports serving London.

Below: One of the best vantage points for sightseeing in London is the top deck of a double-decker bus—seen here passing a mounted sentry at The Horseguards in Whitehall.
Right: The statue of Sir Winston Churchill, war-time Prime Minister and statesman, in a characteristic pose overlooking Westminster.

The London they come to absorbs them remarkably well, even if natives sometimes complain that English is scarcely spoken in summer on No. 11 buses passing Westminster Abbey. London today is a cosmopolitan place; native Londoners increasingly have black, brown or yellow skins rather than white or pink. But immigrants are nothing new. In Spitalfields, just east of the City of London, stand 18th century houses that first gave shelter to Flemish weavers; the nearby building that started as a Lutheran church later served as a synagogue and is now a Bengali mosque. It all makes for vitality and diversity, if also a degree of friction. Dr Johnson's remark about London providing all life can offer, rings even truer today. You can live a lifetime here and still go on discovering something new. As for the ten million tourists — they seem to be able to find more than enough in London to occupy themselves with.

Royal and Traditional London

London is still a royal city, a city of palaces. But for more than two centuries now, British kings and queens have reigned rather than ruled, acting only on the advice of elected governments. London's best-known royal palaces symbolize that constitutional fact. Buckingham Palace, where the Queen lives when in London (if she is there, you see the Royal Standard flying), is, despite a new and grander façade added in 1913, totally eclipsed in grandeur by the Palace of Westminster. And that 19th-century gothic pile between the Thames and Parliament Square, though technically still a royal palace, was built to accommodate the legislature.

There, every autumn, the three branches of Britain's law-making body — Commons, Lords and Sovereign — assemble under one roof for the ceremonial opening of a new session of Parliament. The Queen sits high on her throne; the Lords (some hereditary, some appointed for life) occupy their own benches; the Commons stand. But the speech the Queen reads is written by her Prime Minister, who comes from and commands the support of the elected house, the Commons.

Every year, just before the ceremonial opening, the Serjeant-at-Arms of this still royal palace, in a quaint and symbolic ceremony, leads an armed search of its cellars. He thus recalls the discovery, on November 5th 1605, of kegs of gunpowder in these same underground vaults, intended to blow up King James I, his Ministers and his Parliament. The British custom of bonfires and fireworks each November 5th — Guy Fawkes Day — takes its name from one of the conspirators.

A little more than 600 yards away in Whitehall stands the sole relic of another royal palace, the Palace of Whitehall — its Banqueting House, designed by Inigo Jones and dating from 1622. Here James's son, Charles I, having lost a civil war and been tried for treason, stepped to his execution on a scaffold which was erected just outside these high first-floor windows.

Westminster is royal because the saintly Saxon king, Edward the Confessor, built Westminster Abbey there. The first of the Normans, William the Conqueror, was crowned there in 1066, as has been every crowned British monarch since. The abbey was rebuilt by Henry III (1216-1272); he and five other kings and queen lie buried behind the high altar. When Henry VIII dissolved the monasteries in 1540, the church became a 'Royal Peculiar' independent of any bishop or diocese. Legend has it that John Bradshaw, who pronounced the death sentence on Charles I, haunts the deanery.

Other palaces in central London include St James's — a basically 16th-century building with state apartments by Wren — from whose balcony the Garter King of Arms, England's chief heraldic officer, proclaims new monarchs: Clarence House, home of the Queen Mother; Marlborough House, which accommodates the

The Queen has two birthdays: her actual birthdate, April 21st which is a private and family affair, and her official birthday, in early June, when she reviews her soldiers at the Trooping of the Colour.

Left: The Queen Mother and Princess Anne at the Trooping of the Colour. The stables at Buckingham Palace which looks after carriages and horses is open to the public.
Below: Buckingham Palace, the Queen's London residence, where the Changing of the Guard takes place daily. Visitors can also see changing selections from the royal art collection in the Queen's Gallery.

Commonwealth Secretariat; and Lancaster House, now a conference centre. Here Chopin played to Queen Victoria and Prince Albert; and so grand is the interior that the Queen once told her hostess, the Duchess of Sutherland: 'I have come from my home to your palace!'

Royal ceremonies which the public can see in London include the Changing of the Guard on most days, outside Buckingham Palace and the Horse Guards; the annual Trooping the Colour on the Queen's official birthday in June, when she takes the salute on horseback; and the procession, from Buckingham Palace via the Mall, the Horseguards and Whitehall, for the State Opening of Parliament. Two buildings at Buckingham Palace are open to the public — the Royal Mews, and the Queen's Gallery, which exhibits, in rotation, selections from the interesting and extensive royal art collection.

Ancient and curious ceremonies surrounding the monarchy apart, the most fertile soil for strange and venerable traditions lies in the so-called 'Square Mile' of the City of London. The Lord Mayor, for instance, owes his election not to the Court of Common Council, the elected body which carries out the City's ordinary local government functions, but to the Liverymen of the City Companies — its ancient craft guilds such as Goldsmiths, Fishmongers, Vintners, Cordwainers, Tallowchandlers and 70 or 80 others, some of whose livery halls are among the City's outstanding historic buildings.

These liverymen foregather in Guildhall each Michaelmas Day (September 29th) in quaint and colourful costume including medieval fur-trimmed gowns, and select two aldermen from whom the City's Court of Aldermen (a sort of municipal senate, appointed for life) makes the final choice. Then on the second Saturday in November follows the Lord Mayor's Show, when the newly sworn-in Lord Mayor — in a four-ton 18th-century coach pulled by six horses and with a guard of pikemen in breast plates and helmets — drives to the Law Courts in the Strand to present himself to the Lord Chief Justice.

The Lord Chief Justice represents the Queen; and indeed Lord Mayors used to go by river to Westminster to see the sovereign personally. But now their route lies through crowded City streets, and this symbolic journey has long since become the occasion for a gargantuan procession of tableaux and displays on mobile floats, representing different aspects of City life and centering on a theme nominated by the incoming Lord Mayor.

Another City occasion which combines traditional ceremony with practical, present-day politics is the Lord Mayor's Banquet at Guildhall — one of a number of such occasions every year when guest speakers may include the Prime Minister or the Chancellor of the Exchequer and provide an important opportunity for public exchange of views between the business community and the government of the day. The Lord Mayor in his year of office needs both a fat purse and a strong constitution. He eats countless dinners and delivers more than 1000 speeches in the twelvemonth.

Most famous of his predecessors was Sir Richard Whittington, who as plain Dick Whittington, a lad not yet in his teens, was leaving London when, on Highgate Hill, he heard Bow Bells telling him 'Turn again Whittington, three times Lord Mayor!' In fact he held office four times, and is the popular archetype of the poor boy made good in business. During his year of office the Lord Mayor has precedence within the City boundaries over all save the monarch.

Another ancient tradition, honoured this time just outside the City boundaries, is the Ceremony of the Keys at the Tower of London. When the guard of Yeomen Warders has locked the Tower's outer gate

Left: The King's Troop, Royal
Artillery, fire a salute in Hyde Park
on the Queen's Birthday.
Above: Judges in their wigs and
ceremonial robes walk in procession
to the Royal Courts of Justice in the
Strand at the start of the Legal Year.

each night, returning they meet a sentry. 'Halt, who comes there?' he
challenges. 'The keys', replies the Chief Warder. 'Whose keys?'
demands the sentry. 'Queen Elizabeth's keys', is the reply. At which the
the guard presents arms, the Chief Warder doffs his red and black
Tudor bonnet and pronounces, 'God preserve Queen Elizabeth!'
'Amen!' cry the guard, and march on to lodge the Queen's keys in the
Queen's House, safe within the Inner Ward.

A Thames tradition, Doggett's Coat and Badge, dates from 1715. In
that year Thomas Doggett, actor manager of Drury Lane and a regular
commuter by river from Chelsea, was caught in a storm when he
wanted to go home. A young and impecunious waterman got him
there, so Doggett in gratitude endowed a rowing race for watermen
just out of their apprenticeship. First prize is still 'a Coat of Orange
Livery', a silver badge and a cup. The race takes place in late July or
early August.

The Inns of Court represent a major stronghold of bizarre tradition —
those four walled and gated precincts where barristers, the senior
branch of the English legal profession, who wear wigs and gowns in
court, work together in shared 'chambers', and have their libraries and
dining halls. The Benchers of the four inns — Inner Temple, Middle
Temple, Lincolns Inn and Grays Inn — are judges and senior barristers,
and still exercise the sole right to 'call to the Bar' students who have
qualified for entry into the profession. Examinations apart, a bar
student must still 'keep his terms' by eating so many dinners in hall
each legal term for a number of years. The student who fails to
observe the complex etiquette of these occasions may be fined a bottle
of wine if his neighbour at table challenges his conduct before the
benchers. One bottle of wine for every four students is normally
provided with the meal.

Below: The White Tower, central keep of the Tower of London, was begun by William the Conqueror soon after he took the English throne in 1066.

Right: Ancient customs bring a splash of colour to the workaday city: Life Guards leaving the Mall to return to their barracks after guard duty.

28

Left: The Queen leaves Buckingham Palace to drive to the annual ceremony of the Opening of Parliament. Her speech, though delivered with the Lords seated and the elected Commons standing, is written for her by the Prime Minister with majority support in the elected house.

Below: The Lord Mayor's Show. The incoming Lord Mayor drives in procession through the Square Mile of the City.

Right: The Chelsea Flower Show – an annual riot of colour.

Left: Chelsea Royal Hospital on Founder's Day.
Above: One of the inmates, a Chelsea Pensioner, in his traditional scarlet uniform.

London by Water

London's major highway was traditionally the Thames. That is why two of its greatest palaces, Greenwich and Hampton Court, as well as Westminster and Whitehall, stood on the banks. Greenwich today is not a palace. The splendid group of buildings by Wren, Vanbrugh and Hawksmoor which transform this loop in a generally workaday river have served most of their 250-odd years first as a 'hospital' for naval pensioners, then from 1873 onwards as the Royal Naval College.

Their central vista leads the eye to Greenwich's finest building, Inigo Jones's Queen's House of 1616 — a vista which Wren preserved only on royal insistence. Two colonnades link it to the flanking wings of the National Maritime Museum, of which it now forms part — as does Wren's pretty Flamstead House, built on the hill above for the first Astronomer Royal, Sir John Flamstead.

At this hilltop observatory later Astronomers Royal made the observations which put Greenwich on the map as the Prime Meridian — 0 degrees of longitude—the dividing line between east and west.

By the riverside below stand two famous sailing vessels in a permanent dry-dock: *Cutty Sark,* last of the great clippers that brought tea from the Indies; and *Gypsy Moth,* in which in 1966–1967 Sir Francis Chichester sailed alone round the world.

In central London the great 19th-century granite embankments, added to steadily by new riverside walks, give public access to the Thames; and at two points, Westminster and Charing Cross, river launches, the summer bus service of the tideway — offer regular services downstream to Greenwich, and upstream to Kew, Richmond and Hampton Court. Similar services also run from Tower Pier. They are the best way for a visitor to discover the river. But strollers along the Victoria Embankment can also take pleasure in the growing flotilla of historic vessels permanently moored there. These include Scott's Antarctic exploration ship *Discovery;* a paddle-steamer turned pub, the *Old Caledonia;* and, down river opposite the Tower, *HMS Belfast,* grandly grey, last survivor of a vanished line of steel-hulled, big-gunned 20th-century warships.

One of the delights of a boat trip on the river is its procession of bridges: 27 of them between the Lower Pool, where the docks begin, and Teddington Lock, where the Thames ceases to be tidal. Outstanding among them must be counted Tower Bridge, Victorian gothic on a steel frame and with a central section which still opens for the occasional larger craft; Waterloo, white and clean of line from the 1930s; and Albert, despite its newly inserted central prop, still the prettiest suspension bridge on the tideway. Back below Tower Bridge, St Katharine's Dock, with its old Nore lightship, yacht harbour and splendidly restored ivory warehouse, shows that docks and dock buildings, left redundant by changes in port operations, can yet prove a rich asset to a city.

Further upstream, as the river narrows, come a dozen Thames-side towns and villages, parks and grand houses, preserving their diverse

Despite the movement of port trade down river, the Thames in central London still has its ships – moving and moored. Training ships for sea cadets, Scott's *Discovery,* floating public houses, restaurants, museums and art galleries.

identities in the midst of the London that now surrounds them —
Hurlingham, Fulham Palace, Strand-on-the-Green and Kew; Syon
House; Richmond, Marble Hill and Kingston; Hampton Court and
Molesey — each with its own particular charms and hidden delights.

But London has, apart from the Thames, another and yet more
secret waterway — the Grand Union and Regent canals, constructed in
the late 18th and early 19th centuries to connect the expanding canal
system of the Midlands with the Thames and its docks at Limehouse.
Its best known and most visible stretches are at Little Venice and
alongside the Zoo; also now at Camden Lock. But the Regent canal
mostly hides behind high walls and in deep cuttings — a marvellously
tranquil and attractive 19th-century world which you can explore on
foot along its towpaths (tunnels apart, there is now public access for
most of its length), or better still by boat. Canal 'narrow-boats' of
traditional design offer trips both from Little Venice and Camden Lock;
you can go to the Zoo by boat from Little Venice; and several
restaurant boats offer meals afloat, either moored or moving.

Below: Albert Bridge, between Chelsea and Battersea – arguably London's prettiest bridge.
Right: Ornate Victorian ironwork also gives its own character to the Victoria Embankment at Westminster, but copies of these lampstandards have also been installed on new stretches of river walk on the South Bank.

Lively London

London in the 1970s is an altogether livelier and more cosmopolitan city than anyone could have imagined in the 1950s. The 1960s brought an *avant-garde* consciousness in pop music, pop art and pop fashions in clothes from which the long-standing foreigner's view of England as dull and conventional could never recover.

This 'Swinging London' has continued and grown from strength to strength at at least two focal points. The Carnaby Street area on the Regent Street side of Soho, now freed from traffic and given a psychedelic face-lift by Westminster City Council, offers shoppers a more informal, 'liberated' and, it must be said, noisier alternative to the big department stores of Regent Street and Oxford Street. In Chelsea, the King's Road from Sloane Square westwards into Fulham, full of boutiques, outrageous fashions, roaringly exotic and noisy eating places, *is* an experience — no, an adventure, rather — even for those who go to stare rather than buy.

The informality and non-conformity encouraged by the Swinging 1960s has spread, in a diluted, less garish form, into every aspect of London life. Matching it is the incredible cosmopolitanism of the city. In the London of the 1930s, the first Italian restaurant seemed, to the insular citizens of those days, exotic and suspect. Now in central London you can find Japanese, Hungarian, Burmese, Mexican, Scandinavian, Greek, Spanish, French, Italian, Dutch and many other nationalities of eating places; while almost every suburb has its Chinese and Indian take-aways and kebab-houses.

Londoners, too, are now a cosmopolitan crowd. China Town, originally in Limehouse, has now established itself round Gerrard Street in Soho — the district which still possesses the biggest and most polyglot concentration of exotic eating places, even if now marginally threatened for space by the spread of the blue film and pornography merchants.

Camden Town and Kentish Town have long been the Greek Cypriot quarter; New Cross is strong in Turks; Bengalis have colonised Spitalfields, as European Jews and Flemish weavers did before them; and Brixton and Notting Hill are the most notable centres of London's big West Indian population.

Each celebrates its distinctive customs and festivities — paper dragons and fire crackers in Soho; colourful saints' day processions at St Cyprians, Kentish Town; and — biggest, gayest but sometimes unhappily tinged with minority violence — the intensely colourful and noisy carnivals of the Caribbean communities.

London is on the whole an easy-going city. Policemen do not arrest you for crossing the road when the traffic light says 'Wait' to pedestrians. It's left to your good sense. Park keepers do not pursue you for walking or lying on grass. That, they say, is what it's there for — unless they have just resown it with grass-seed, in which case they'll fence it off.

Greek Street in Soho. Soho is still London's most cosmopolitan village, offering the most exciting range of places in which to eat out, and still has the best streets in London for food shops.

Londoners don't like their town to be *too* tidy, as indeed town planners discovered when public opinion killed successive schemes for 'redeveloping' the cheerful visual anarchy of Piccadilly Circus. Sensible improvements like the pedestrianizing of Leicester Square, with its extra benches, trees and flower-beds, they applaud.

Young London often seems a city in blue jeans. The town has its elegant streets and quarters, but for the most part people prefer it to be, not smart and conformist, but interesting and agreeable.

Above: London has always been a
centre for music of all kinds. 'The
Ants' are a New Wave band seen
here playing at the Royal College of
Art.
Right: Slightly less avant-garde
musicians, Garth Hewitt and Kenny
Marks at The Upstream Club in
Waterloo.

Pearly Kings and Queens are a long
established tradition. Originally they
were a typical Cockney device to
bring colour and gaiety to drab,
impoverished London streets.
Nowadays they help raise money for
charity.

Far left: Carnaby Street was a focal point of 1960's 'Swinging London'. It helped London become a rival to Paris in the fashion markets of the world, and is still a Mecca for overseas visitors.
Left and below: The West Indians, who migrated to London in the '50s and '60s, brought a new vitality and sense of colour which they express in the now annual Notting Hill Carnival.

Cultural London

The English traditionally distrust 'culture' as a concept and avoid using the word cultural. But that has not stopped their capital city from offering a more extravagant cultural banquet than almost anywhere else in the world.

One very richly laden platter is the South Bank riverside complex. Here stand three concert halls: the Royal Festival Hall, the Queen Elizabeth Hall and the smaller, more intimate Purcell Room; three theatres: Olivier, Lyttelton and Cottesloe, all part of Sir Denys Lasdun's exciting and impressive National Theatre building; two cinemas: the National Theatre's NFT One and NFT Two showing a variety of foreign, classic and off-beat films not usually seen in the commercial cinema; and for limited-period art exhibitions, the Hayward Gallery.

Central London's theatre-and-cinema-land also offers a remarkable feast. The two London evening newspapers regularly list some 70 theatres and as many central area cinemas. The heart of theatreland remains Shaftesbury Avenue and Covent Garden; most theatres there mount whatever plays or 'shows' producers think can make money. But in addition to the subsidized National Theatre, we find several other 'non-commercial' repertory companies — outstandingly, the Royal Shakespeare company at the Aldwych, but also the Royal Court in Chelsea's Sloane Square; the Mermaid, built in the shell of a Thames Warehouse at Puddle Dock, Blackfriars; the St George's, Tufnell Park, a Victorian church skilfully converted into a theatre of Shakespeare's day, and such local companies as Greenwich, whose high standards ensure that many of its productions transfer to the West End.

Art galleries and museums, too, offer themselves in profusion. The National Gallery in Trafalgar Square is pre-eminent in old masters; the Tate in impressionists; the Victoria and Albert, that rich and varied treasure-house in South Kensington, must not be missed by any devotee of the decorative arts. The Royal Academy at Burlington House, Piccadilly, stages regular definitive exhibitions on individual artists and subjects; hidden behind it in Burlington Gardens is the not-to-be missed Museum of Mankind.

South Kensington is London's traditional 'museum-land', established with the profits of the 1851 Great Exhibition. As well as the 'V & A', here stand the imaginatively presented Geological Museum; the Science Museum (really more a museum of technology); and, with its great halls full of whale and dinosaur skeletons, the British Museum of Natural History. South Kensington, grandly Victorian in architecture and in earnest pursuit of knowledge, also contains the Royal Albert Hall — London's most magnificent if never its best concert hall; and the Albert Memorial once abused by the 1950s 'anti-uglies', but now an object of affectionate wonder.

Kenwood House, its landscaped grounds merging with Hampstead Heath, was rebuilt by Robert Adam in the 1760s. Left to the nation by the Earl of Iveagh, it provides a splendid setting for a valuable collection of paintings and art treasures, as well as for concerts and recitals.

Further east, in Bloomsbury, stands the greatest treasure-house of all, the British Museum. Between it and Kings Cross, where a new British Library building is to be constructed, lies the academic precinct of London University. In the City, the Barbican Arts Centre is slowly taking shape, in a bombed quarter where new homes and new cultural ferment are intended to lighten the dead hours and days when the Square Mile's office workers have almost all fled to the suburbs.

Left: The new Museum of London at Barbican houses the combined collections of the former Guildhall and London museums. This cell, from an 18th century prison is one of the exhibits.

Above: A scene from the Royal Shakespeare Company's revival of 'Wild Oats', a 19th century comedy by John O'Keefe.

Overleaf: A magnificent scene from the Royal Ballet's production of 'Swan Lake' at the Royal Opera House, Covent Garden.

Left: The concrete and glass conglomeration of London's cultural centre on the South Bank of the Thames. Here there is a cinema complex, an art gallery and three concert halls. The futuristic landscape was also the birthplace of skateboarding in England, where young enthusiasts found the architect's concrete dream was perfect for their new sport.

Below: Sunday's open-air art exhibition along the park railings at Lancaster Gate.

London's Green Spaces

Air passengers passing over central London often express surprise at how much green there is in the city below them. For London is generously if patchily endowed with parks, squares and gardens and more than one-tenth of its 390000 acres is public open space, or almost 6 acres for every 1000 of its resident population.

This generous endowment of open space is in part the result of Tudor monarchs' hunting habits. The chain of royal parks (public, but administered for the Crown by the Department of the Environment) were mostly in origin places to hunt deer. Stuart and later monarchs had them landscaped into parks in our modern sense and then threw them open to their subjects.

The Royal Parks include not only St James's with its lake and ornamental ducks, geese and wildfowl; Green Park, an oasis of verdure behind the traffic maelstrom of Hyde Park Corner; Hyde Park, with its riders in Rotten Row and its boating and swimming at the Serpentine; and Kensington Gardens with its Round Pond and elfin oak; but also Regents Park, bordered by Nash terraces and its adjunct to the north, Primrose Hill.

The Greater London Council also provides some fine expanses of parkland, outstanding among them Hampstead Heath and its associated open spaces, with picture galleries, open air concerts and a duelling ground at Kenwood; kite flying on Parliament Hill; and on the heath itself fairs, pleasant walks and the illusion of endless countryside. Other parts of London enjoy a profusion of smaller parks commons and woods open to the public. These include Blackheath, above Greenwich; and Clapham and Wimbledon Commons in the south. To the south-east the GLC also maintains a chain of upland woods and commons leading down to the Thames at Lesnes Abbey, the ruins of an Augustinian foundation, which now look out over London's own riverside new town of Thamesmead. In Abbey Woods bloom daffodils said to be descendants of those planted there by the medieval monks.

Two of London's largest and most popular open spaces are, paradoxically, maintained by the City Corporation outside not only its own narrow boundaries but those of Greater London – Burnham Beeches in Buckinghamshire; and Epping Forest, which is largely in Essex – a long chain of forest jutting into north-east London.

One special open space is the London Zoo, straddling the Regent Canal on the northern edges of Regent's Park. It holds 7000 wild animals; is administered by the Zoological Society of London; and in recent years alongside the original charming animal houses of the 1820s and 1930s stand larger modern buildings, functional and with exciting rooflines, such as Lord Snowdon's aviary and Casson, Condor & Partners evocative elephant houses.

Richmond Park is perhaps the most rural of the great Royal Parks, though by no means the only one with a herd of deer.

Left: The statue of Peter Pan, the boy who never grew up, created by the author J. M. Barrie and a firm favourite with children even today.
Below: A favourite pastime of Londoners is feeding the ducks in the park. London's Royal Parks are the accidental heritage of a series of royal hunting forests.

Below: The perfect escape from the hectic city rush; boating in Regent's Park, only minutes from the West End.

Below right: Polar bears are just one of the multitude of creatures to be found in London Zoo, which skirts Regent's Park on its north side.

Left: Rotten Row, traditionally the fashionable London ride along the southern edge of Hyde Park, is now paralleled by a new cycle path.
Right: Speaker's Corner, near Marble Arch is the traditional venue for the Englishman to exercise his right of freedom of speech. Here an anarchist preaches his esoteric gospel.
Below: The many-pinnacled Whitehall/Westminster skyline seen from St James's Park.

Old London

London the 20th-century workaday city has much that survives from previous centuries – but in different degrees and at different levels. At one extreme we can find individual buildings – a City livery hall or a Wren church here, a 17th-century merchant's house there – whose form and fabric seem to have survived virtually unchanged. Then come bigger pockets or islands of antiquity where, again, the 20th-century scarcely seems to encroach. Narrow, traffic-free Goodwins Court, an almost hidden alley off St Martin's Lane with its unaltered 200-year-old shop fronts and houses, is one example.

A group of houses at Smithfield, 39–45 Cloth Fair provide, scarcely a butcher's hook away from the bustling modern meat market, the momentary illusion that we are in 17th-century London; Westminster Hall within the Houses of Parliament, with its great hammer-beam roof and stone austerity of floor and wall, still half seems to echo with the legal Latin and Norman French phrases of Tudor judges. New Square in Lincoln's Inn, spacious, tranquil and 17th century in its rhythms of stucco and brick, could be the place where Charles Dickens worked as an office boy.

In the Temple, to the south across Fleet Street we find a whole series of courts and lanes, halls, houses, chambers and chapels which look a good 300–400 years old even where the Benchers have had to patch and adapt.

Mostly, though, London's oldness is more diluted: antiquity has had to come to terms with the modern city. At this level whole quarters of London clearly rank as 'old' both for their architecture and, also, for a sense of style, an atmosphere which somehow survives tarmac road surfaces, motor vehicles and modern street lighting. Outstanding are the great landed estates developed in a spacious, well-mannered way in the 18th and early 19th centuries – St James, Bloomsbury, Belgravia, Mayfair and Marylebone among them.

The pattern the Georgians and earlier Victorians preferred was a largely rectilinear street plan softened by squares and crescents, planted with trees and shrubs but carefully railed and gated against the vulgar *plebs*. It is these squares and gardens – some now public, others still reserved for residents – which, with their well proportioned classical architecture and their welcome greenery are the chief glory of large swathes of Inner London.

For the devotee of Pepys or Johnson or even Dickens, a pilgrimage in pursuit of the famous shade is indeed a will-o'-the-wisp undertaking. Most of the houses they lived in have vanished, though Dr Johnson's House at Gough Square survives (a fine and interesting building in itself), as does Dickens' home from 1837–1839 in Doughty Street, Holborn, where he worked away at at least three major novels: *The Pickwick Papers, Oliver Twist* and *Nicholas Nickleby*. The George and Vulture in the City still provides the venue for a latter-day Pickwick Club; and across the river in Southwark, the George gives a glimpse of the kind of galleried courtyard typical of the many now-vanished coaching inns.

The bas-reliefs at the foot of Nelson's Column. Erected in 1839-42, the Column is made of Devon granite, and is 170 feet tall. It is topped by a 16 foot statue of Admiral Nelson.

Back across London Bridge the Monument is worth the labour of climbing its 311 steps for the view it still gives over Thames and City. It is 202 feet high, and marks the distance from the spot in a baker's shop in Pudding Lane where the Great Fire of London began in 1666. The lanes and alleys to the east, round Lovat Lane and St Mary-at-Hill, form one of the few surviving fragments of the old merchant City.

Left: St Martin's-in-the-Fields'
church was once just what its name
suggests – in the fields beyond the
western boundary of the City of
London. Now Gibb's classical 18th
century church is a focal point of
Trafalgar Square, the official centre
of London from which road-sign
distances are measured. The statue
in the foreground is the Duke of
Wellington.
Above: The Whitehall skyline as
seen from Trafalgar Square.

Left: The Royal Courts of Justice in the Strand, usually called simply 'The Law Courts'. This 19th century gothic group of buildings designed by G. E. Streek houses only the High Court's civil cases. Criminal cases are heard at the Old Bailey.
Below: Henekey's Long Bar, next to the gateway of Gray's Inn, is a favourite haunt of lawyers and law students.
Right: St James's Palace includes some of the 16th century buildings which Henry VIII constructed on the site of 'the Hospital of St James for leper maidens'.

Below: Admiralty Arch is the ceremonial gateway from Trafalgar Square into the long processional route of the Mall up to Buckingham Palace – all a memorial to Queen Victoria.
Right: The cloisters of Westminster Abbey, which date from the 13th century.
Below right: The beautifully vaulted cloister roof.

London Villages

When we talk of London villages, we may mean any one of a number of different things. First there is the picturesque surviving village centre, church and churchyard, winding high street, charmingly crooked group of cottages and perhaps stately manor house, embedded in the fabric and life of a busy suburb when once it stood amid fields and woods.

Charlton in south-east London is a good example of this type of village, though its surroundings are now marred by the oppressive presence of large, barrack-like blocks of municipal flats on the hillside below. Still, thanks to the efforts of an active local civic society, Charlton is now looking very pretty. It has its 17th-century brick church, whose churchyard has lately been given a discreet facelift; its high street with a charming pub, the Bugle Horn; mounts an annual Horn Fair, revived after a century or so; and a stately Jacobean manor house, now used as library and community centre, whose Dutch gabled stable-block has recently been restored and converted to office and community use.

Charlton is not famous among London villages; one and a half miles beyond Greenwich, it is off the tourist track. It lacks the social cachet of Hampstead, Highgate, or Blackheath. These, with Chelsea in the central area, and Dulwich and perhaps Wimbledon to the south, represent a second kind of village: one whose ancient village centre is physically preserved, but where fashion has wrought a profound social and commercial change.

Restaurants, antique shops and boutiques have gradually taken over from less profitable, but from the residents' point of view, often more useful, shops; the place is a-bustle not so much with local people as with visitors who come to eat, drink, explore the antique shops and boutiques and generally just stroll about and enjoy agreeable surroundings and a stimulating atmosphere.

More numerous is the ordinary run of villages, local centres with shops and cinemas, churches, libraries and often a town hall or community centre. Frequently the commuter station is the focus. Other London villages such as Kew have two distinct centres, the village round the green, and the Victorian village centre built in the 1860s and 1870s round the station.

Some local centres are recognizably 'towns' rather than 'villages'. Woolwich, for instance, or Uxbridge, on the western edge of London. And then, close to Uxbridge we find, finally, a fourth type of village.

Harefield, set in the green belt and still workaday and agricultural, has never been fashionable. It is a 'mud-on-your-boots' village rather than a pretty, pink-gin commuter village. Much of the land hereabouts is actually owned by the Greater London Council, and at least one GLC tenant farmer opens his farm to the public several days each year.

Townsmen who live cheek-by-jowl with the countryside, he says, need to be shown how it works so that they respect it. The GLC agrees and encourages such farm open days.

The city still has its fragments of riverside villages, tranquil and unspoiled oases amidst the rush and roar of modern London. Here, Strand-on-Green, with its boats, pubs and attractive waterside houses.

Left: Gentleman's Walk, Enfield – an elegant district.

Right: Bedford Park, a model suburb laid out in later Victorian times for middle-class families with artistic pretensions and glorying in leafy tree-lined avenues and stylish red-brick houses by such architects as Norman Shaw.

Below: Highgate Village, with its hilltop high street, has kept its character and identity despite being split, for municipal purposes, between three different boroughs.

Highgate and Hampstead are twin villages on the Northern Heights, with the carefully cultivated 'wildscape' of Hampstead Heath between them.
Left: open-air drinkers at the Flask public house in Highgate Village.
Right: Hampstead Fair, a regular Bank Holiday event for Londoners.
Below: One of the many ponds which give the Heath much of its character. Who would think this scene is only 15 minutes or so by the Underground from the heart of the West End?

Markets and Emporiums

Shopping in London runs the whole gamut from the elegant and expensive specialist shops of Bond Street, St James, and Saville Row to bustling Cockney street markets like Petticoat Lane and Chapel Market in Islington.

One of the prettiest and most elegant places to shop is Burlington Arcade. It is sedately 1820s in style, covered against the rain and very expensive. There is still a uniformed beadle who restrains anyone tempted to do so unseemly a thing as *run*. Legend has it that some years ago he effectively restrained a public-spirited citizen running in pursuit of a thief.

Saville Row, the street of tailors, has this same aura of expensive elegance, as does Old Bond Street with its jewellers and picture galleries, and St James with its old-established wine merchants and shoe-makers, exclusive and urbane behind their inviting, yet ostentatious, 18th-century shop-fronts.

Harrods, of course, is the best known of the great emporiums – a department store whose boast is that it will sell you almost anything. Most Londoners prefer the less expensive stores such as John Lewis, Selfridges, or for clothes Fenwicks, Austin Reed or one of the large stores of Oxford and Regent Streets.

For design and quality, Liberty's behind its 1920s half-timbering, and Heal's are among the leaders; for 'with it' household goods and furnishings the various branches of Habitat are beyond compare. For high quality edible English goodies Jackson's in Picadilly and its neighbour Fortnum & Mason (with a miniature Mr Fortnum and Mr Mason as bellboys to strike the hour for the clock outside) beckon compellingly. In Jermyn Street behind them, Paxton & Whitfield stocks a range of cheeses to throw the gourmet into ecstasies. For umbrellas (also sword-sticks and shooting sticks), James Smith & Sons on the corner of New Oxford Street and Shaftsbury Avenue is *the* place.

As for street markets, the two most famous are Petticoat Lane, the traditional and longstanding Sunday morning general and rag-trade market held in Middlesex Street, near Aldgate on the eastern edge of the City; and Portobello Road, the antique and junk Mecca frequented by wealthy tourists, in north Kensington.

London's wholesale markets can also be fun to look at, though in the interests of efficient operation they increasingly discourage outsiders. Covent Garden, trading fruit and vegetables across the pavement in the heart of the West End, used to be the great draw, full of noise, bustle and the smell of decaying cabbage; but the New Covent Garden Market at Nine Elms is enclosed, mechanized, efficient, and excludes the public altogether. At Spitalfields and the Borough, trading still spills out of doors across pavements; as it does at Smithfield (meat) and Billingsgate (fish).

But trade involves retail as well as wholesale. Thus a large area of north London is learning to appreciate the advantages of motorized, one-stop shopping at Brent Cross, a huge brick box at the intersection of the M1 motorway and the North Circular Road, surrounded by car parks and containing branches of many major stores. As enclosed shopping centres go, this is quite a good one, with attractive 'open' cafés in the main shopping mall and some interior sense of style and atmosphere. Not as lively as a street market, but useful.

Souvenirs for tourists bring colour and vitality to the pavements of London.

Don't Squeeze Me
'Till I'm Yours

Antiques, 'sub-antiques', junk – the whole business of second-hand goods with the attraction of age has boomed in London in recent years.
Above: Portobello Road, Mecca of the popular antique world.
Right: A busker with an unusual line in entertainment.
Far right: 'Be a dear and raise your hats to the readers!'

Left: Harrods, which will supply almost anything, at a price.
Below: Wray's Lighting Emporium has 'rubbed up' the traditional shop-front character of the King's Road admirably.
Below right: Habitat is one of the new Aladdin's Caves of the London retail scene.

Sporting London

London as a centre for spectator sports has much to offer. In the football season there are a dozen professional clubs to choose from: Arsenal and Tottenham Hotspur in the north; Brentford, Chelsea, Fulham and Queen's Park Rangers in the West; Crystal Palace, Millwall and Charlton in the south; Leyton Orient and West Ham United in the east; and Watford on London's northern fringe. Wembley Stadium, which holds 100000 spectators under cover, is the venue for international matches and for the top domestic fixture, the Cup Final.

What Wembley is to soccer, Twickenham is to Rugby Union. Harlequins, who play there, are one of 11 leading Rugby Union clubs in London. The English national summer game of cricket has its headquarters at Lord's in St John's Wood, headquarters of both the ruling body, the MCC, and of a leading county, Middlesex. The other main cricket ground in London is the Oval, where Surrey plays.

The Mecca of lawn tennis is, of course, Wimbledon, where the All England Club have recently opened a fascinating museum of the history of the game; just as Hurlingham is the sedate and private headquarters of the game of croquet.

For athletics, the national and international venue is now, for the most part, the National Sports Centre at Crystal Palace. It is set in a park which surrounds the site of Paxton's revolutionary iron-and-glass exhibition building of 1851 – alas, burnt down in 1936. Big boxing matches usually take place at either Wembley or the Royal Albert Hall; horse racing in season at Sandown Park, Kempton Park, Epsom Downs and Windsor.

Participatory as distinct from spectator sport is well catered for in two ways: clubs and public facilities. Swimming pools abound; there are tennis courts in almost every public park. In fine weather the lakes in Regent's and Hyde parks are covered with boats.

Recent years have, however, seen a certain change of emphasis, with deliberately growing provision for the 'non-joiner'. Thus the Lee Valley Regional Park Pickett's Lock Centre, with swimming pool and covered and open-air sports facilities, seeks specifically to encourage informal recreation, especially in family groups, rather than conventional competitive sports.

The Lee Valley Park, spread over 19 miles of the neglected, down-at-heel flood plain of the River Lee in north east London, aims to improve all manner of recreational facilities for that traditionally under-provided sector of London. With its expanding provision for boating, swimming, horse-riding, walking, running, and indeed just sitting and dreaming in pleasant surroundings, it is London's most ambitious recreational experiment to date.

Of all the London race meetings, Royal Ascot – which the Queen and members of her family traditionally attend – is the most fashionable. Grey top hats, strawberries and cream, and much pomp and circumstance is the order of the day. The thousands of more ordinary racegoers who gaze at the occupants of the Royal Enclosure, do so these days more with amused tolerance than with envy.

Below: To the casual observer, croquet often seems a game of unruffled tranquillity. However, it does have its moments of viciousness and its times for vengeance.

Right: Veteran motor cars cross Westminster Bridge at the start of the annual London to Brighton Rally.

Right: One of London's top class football teams, Queen's Park Rangers, playing at their home ground against Manchester City.
Top, far right: Borg and Nastase battle it out at the Wimbledon Tennis Championships.
Bottom, far right: The Mile field slogging it out at the Crystal Palace sports centre.

Changing London

In one sense, London has changed more in the last 25 years than in all its 20 centuries. It has changed in vertical scale. Firm planning policies have indeed stopped its sprawl. Instead of growing outwards it has grown upwards. The City of London has sprouted a score of tall towers, bursting the 100 foot height limit long maintained by the old London County Council, swamping that incomparable skyline of Wren spires, and in effect shrinking St Paul's whose dome no longer dominates as it did for 250 years.

In the West End, the illusion the royal parks once fostered that you were in the heart of the countryside, has gone. Elegant though it may be, the Knightsbridge Barracks tower blows one more hole in that illusion, first damaged by the early 1960s London Hilton.

The Post Office Tower, that cheerfully vulgar symbol of a changing West End (bulging with radio link transmitters for our telephone system and a revolving restaurant), is now challenged for height by the new National Westminster Bank tower rising above the City. We have to look hard now for poor old St Paul's.

All this, of course, is an expression of the commercial City seeking to modernize and expand its working space within the tight limits of the Square Mile. However, the developers do not have their own way the whole time. Even late Victorian and early 20th-century commercial buildings are now statutorily protected and occasionally, despite the millions of pounds at stake, Government Ministers, on the advice of public inquiry inspectors, rule that they are too precious and have too much historical importance to demolish.

Conservation and concern for good environment now dominate the thinking of London's town planners. Architects tend more and more to favour sympathetic infill development rather than brash or arrogantly modern design to fill gaps in an older townscape. The paving over of Leicester Square and many other sections of street in both central London and the suburbs represents a new sensitivity to the needs of pedestrians as against motorists.

During the early 1970s London's voters effectively stopped for good the building of large-scale, expensive and ruinously destructive urban motorways in inner London. An outer ring, the M25 orbital motorway, is however pressing ahead at a radius of some 12–15 miles from the centre, aimed at taking the bulk of bypassable traffic, especially heavy container lorries from the industrial Midlands to the Channel ports, out of the streets of London.

That and new measures to revitalize the more down-at-heel inner city areas are the biggest changes currently taking place. For now London clearly perceives that 'quality of life' depends on more than simply concrete, steel and glass, or bricks and mortar. Reasonable prosperity and a stable, pleasing environment are now recognized as the cornerstones of contentment.

The tunnel of the new Fleet Line underground railway during construction. This is the first stage of the new line running from Charing Cross to Baker Street, where it links with the existing Stanmore branch of the Bakerloo Line.

Below: The redevelopment of the north side of Victoria Street in the 1960s was a disaster of dullness. The total opposite is the '70s development on the south side by architects Elsom, Pack and Roberts, who have brought a distinctive and mildly jokey character to enliven the scene.
Right: One of an epidemic of large new hotels encouraged by generous government grants in the 1960s.

Above: The Nash terraces formed
the traditional delicate backcloth to
Regent's Park, until the arrival of the
new London Mosque and Islamic
Centre designed by Sir Frederick
Gibberd and sited at Hanover Gate.
Right: The interior of the new Brent
Cross shopping centre, showing the
ornamental fountain and spectacular
coloured glass roof.

Above: The Hilton Hotel in Park Lane – at first regarded by Londoners as an out-of-scale intruder; now almost an old friend.

Right: The old and the new rub shoulders, the Old Curiosity Shop, said to have links with Charles Dickens, in a side street between Lincolns Inn Fields and the London School of Economics.

Far right: The new glass facades of London offices tower above the more friendly equivalent of a past era.

London Excursions

The best way to reach Kew is by boat up river from Westminster or Charing Cross piers. Kew began as a park surrounding a royal palace, but unlike other such royal parks never became a *public* open space. Instead it forms the Royal Botanic Gardens, whose prime purpose is to advance the science of botany.

The gardens contain some 45000 different trees and plants. The Herbarium, not ordinarily open to the public, is, in effect, a huge filing cabinet containing some seven million dried plants and herbs.

Exotic buildings as well as exotic flora beguile your wanderings through the gardens – the pagoda, the Palm House, the Temperate House and the charming little Kew Palace or Dutch House of 1631, with its newly created Elizabethan herb garden behind it.

By the same boat as to Kew you can normally reach Hampton Court, the 16th-century palace built by Henry VIII's rich and powerful chancellor Thomas Wolsey. Its very grandeur accelerated Wolsey's downfall, which the gift of Hampton Court to the king failed to avert. Henry added to it as did other monarchs after him: Wren added the fountain court and state apartments for William and Mary. Hampton Court Park and the adjoining Bushy Park spaciously accommodate Versailles-like vistas. The palace's attractions include its Tudor kitchens, state apartments, the Great Vine, the Maze, and the huge and finely decorated 16th-century Astronomical Clock above Anne Boleyn's Gateway.

Another Tudor palace in all but name is Knole, the ancestral seat of the Sackville family since 1603 – though its earliest buildings date from 1456. Now owned by the National Trust, it is said to contain a room for every day of the year and a staircase for every week.

Knole's main drive runs about half-a-mile straight out of the centre of the charming Kentish town of Sevenoaks; the extensive park with its herds of deer then stretches to the edge of the wooded Greens and hills. With its great ragstone walls and curling Tudor chimneys, its outbuildings housing granaries, bakery, brewery, blacksmith's and stables, Knole is more like a self-contained medieval town than a mansion. Walks in the park are a delight. Sevenoaks is about 35 minutes by rail from Charing Cross or Victoria.

Brighton, only 55 minutes by train from Victoria, is London's most popular and stylish seaside resort. Not to be missed are the curiously oriental Royal Pavilion, the stately terraces of Kemp Town and Hove and the Lanes, a network of narrow shopping streets between the town centre and the seafront.

North of London on the edge of the Chiltern Hills lies Whipsnade, more spacious country branch of the London Zoo. Here the animals are, so to speak, in the open, in wide paddocks; the visitors confined to the spaces in between. Sometimes humans and other mammals are allowed to mix, as on the downland edge of the zoological park where wallabys hop wild as well as other smaller creatures. A minibus service provides transport for those unable or unwilling to walk around this extensive park.

Windsor Castle, a medieval fortress turned into a royal residence. Its hunting forests are now wonderfully landscaped parks open to the public. The castle is seen here from the Long Walk.

Windsor Castle, farther up river from Hampton Court, is the Queen's chief country residence, built originally by William the Conqueror but much added to over the centuries. St George's Chapel, with its stalls of the Order of Knights of the Garter and fine fan-vaulted roof, stands within the castle. To its west and south stretch the twin expanses of Windsor Home and Great parks; close under its walls on the east is the town of Windsor with its 17th-century Guildhall, stately houses and attractive riverside. Across the now pedestrians-only Windsor Bridge lies Eton's narrow and historic high street and Eton College, founded by Henry VI in 1440. The Royal Windsor Horse Show takes place each Spring; Windsor Safari Park lies two miles to the south-west.

North of London, 30-40 minutes by train from Moorgate or King's Cross, lies Hatfield House, built in the 17th century for Robert Cecil, first Earl of Salisbury. It is Jacobean architecture at its most sumptuous. Here the second Marquis, around 1850, welcomed the railways, unlike most other landed proprietors of that era, but required the Great Northern Railway Company to lengthen its platform at Hatfield Station and provide him with a private waiting room.

Left: the Royal Horticultural Society's gardens at Wisley, just south-west of London.
Below left: Brighton's bizarre Royal Pavilion, built for a Prince Regent.
Below: Epping Forest, a chain of woodland penetrating right into east London, where the visitor can actually escape on two legs from the tyranny of four wheels!

Left: Kew Gardens, an unrivalled collection of trees and plants in a landscape dotted with beautiful and bizarre buildings, like this 18th-century pagoda.
Right: Epping Forest is wilder. Queen Elizabeth's Hunting Lodge recalls Tudor times when it was a royal hunting forest rather than a Londoner's playground.
Below right: Hampton Court, too, began as a Tudor palace, but the landscape gardening is of a later, more elegant age when French influences were strong. This shows the Sunken Garden.